# Specialist Nation

A Survival Guide For America

Doug O'Bryon

**Editorial Reviews**

**Crispin Cruz, Corporate Vice President of Sales, MaximusJobs**

Who is this book for? A better question is, "Who is this book NOT for!" Brilliant, compelling, storytelling. An engaging combination of objective thought-leadership insights and state-of-the-union pragmatism, all wrapped in O'Bryon's signature tongue-in-cheek style.

**Pamela Atwood, President, Atwood Associates**

"Coming from the staffing industry, I am recommending this book for both candidates and clients, for the simple reason that it would save me countless hours of explaining to them why these rapid and radical changes are occurring within education, employment, and the economy, and how best position individuals to succeed. This book should be required reading for everyone 16 to 60."

**Jack Gabriel, Founder, The Provato Group**

In the interest of full disclosure, I've been a fan of the author since his 2008 book, "*Banks, Tanks &Angst: How Long will America Idle?*" when he stared down Dow 13,750 and warned of a market crash, followed by 3-5 years of economic turmoil he coined,

"Lagflation," and since then over 15 of his specific predictions have come true. Now he's at it again, with an insightful and impassioned manifesto pleading for change in America's educational and economic ecosystem – trailblazing a national reorientation from generalist to specialist – and thereby maximizing the full impact of what he has coined our "Productivity Dividend."

## Steve Rucinski, Ricoh Americas Corporation

Doug is fearless, speaking truth to power. In a single book, he takes on the entrenched thinking in athletics, academics, global corporate strategy, the Harvard Business Review – even the future of American exceptionalism – and WINS! Anyone can complain about the complexity of our nationwide struggles with unemployment, education, student loans, skills gaps, and outsourcing, but he's one of the few to actually tackle these challenges head-on and offer real workable bipartisan solutions.

## Vincent K. Roach, CEO Business Intelligence, Inc.

Once again, Doug O'Bryon tackles a huge problem and nails the solution in a few choice and entertaining words. In this compact blueprint, he chronicles the struggle of both the American worker and the American economy, as they seek to successfully navigate the galloping technological changes of our new global competition, and how this impacts the achievement of the American Dream. Billions of words and millions of speeches have confused the hearer and discouraged the seekers, yet in a few elegant and easy-to-grasp pages, O'Bryon lays out the problem and provides direction to all.

This book could save untold hours of talk, worry, and confusion, if only our advisors & experts, teachers & guidance counselors, policy wonks & cabinet members were to zip their mouths, pitch out all their tired PhD theses, and instead hand this book to our youth, their teachers, and each other. Simply put, all who struggle to find meaningful and prosperous work in today's economy are well advised to think deeply about what Doug has to say.

**Preface**

To: My children Grant and Audrey

From: Dad

Dear Kids:

I'm afraid I have some bad news. The America you are growing up in is not the America I grew up in.

When I grew up, there were 200 million people in America, and 3.5 billion people in the world. Now there are over 300 million Americans and over 7 billion people in the world – and as of right now, you're competing with ALL of them to eke out a living in our integrated "global workforce" economy.

But it gets worse. Your "world class" educational system (which is supposed to prepare you to successfully compete in this marketplace) is still trapped in the 60's – prioritizing pedagogy and curating curriculum as if nothing has changed – and churning out class after class of unemployable graduates destined for a life of financial flotsam drowning in a sea of student debt.

And here's the kicker. Nobody "out there" seems to get it. So far, all of the challenges awaiting you are being addressed by the government, media, and academia as single-issue problems existing within discrete industry silos and/or specific situational contexts (e.g. skills gap, insourcing, student debt, unemployment, etc.), with each entity informing their opinions with the requisite spin of their party, provost, or positional bias…which is why I decided to write this book.

As your Dad, I have no hidden agenda, nor any outstanding stocks, positions, or holdings in any of the institutions enclosed. Instead, my interest is in seeing you – and every other teenager, young adult, and seasoned worker – succeed, and in doing so, collectively help to return America to her exceptional roots and place of commercial and industrial prominence on the world stage. Consider this book your Survival Guide, because in many ways, it is.

The book you are about to read is SHORT for three reasons. One, because you're busy. Two, because you have a short attention span. And three, because I wanted to make sure you actually FINISH the book – because it has a hopeful ending. If you invest the 30 minutes to complete this book you will finally understand – not only the WHAT of our current situation as individuals and as a nation, but also the WHY – for only when you understand WHY can you begin to make the right choices for strategically positioning yourself for success by choosing to SPECIALIZE as an athlete, academic, and American at the dawn of this new era.

Just like the "Productivity Dividend" concept introduced and explored in the coming pages, the challenges facing America today are interconnected, systemic, and structural, requiring integrated, systemic, and structural solutions. I know you think of social anthropology and economic theory as boring and irrelevant, so I have included as many pop culture references as possible – linking running backs to the Renaissance, tractors to trade schools, org charts to depth charts, Guiding Stars to movie stars, and Apple to America – to characterize our problems and offer practical and pragmatic solutions for our current situation. Just as *Seinfeld* integrated an array of plot lines to elevate comedic storytelling into a symphony of ironic intertwined jokes, it is the 50,000-foot "big picture" storyline connecting all of these dots (in support of an argument towards specialization) that provides the pattern recognition platform for explaining what comes next and how to specialize – and thereby thrive – in this environment.

I know this letter is already longer than your Tweets, texts, and blogs, so in case this Preface is all you read, let me summarize with this thought. **A Decathlete who comes in 2nd in all ten events will win a Gold Medal, but a job seeker who comes in 2$^{nd}$ ten times when competing for a job is still unemployed.**

The message for you and for athletes, academics, companies and countries is clear. The world no longer prefers a Swiss Army Knife – they want a drawer full of knives, each uniquely designed for a specific task.

**Your mother was right.** You ARE special. Now act like it.

Love,

Dad

## Introduction

**Last summer, the gaze of the globe** was focused on London to watch the 2012 version of the quadrennial five-ring-circus known as the Olympics – while providing the United Kingdom one last chance to show us exactly what makes Britain so Great.

The red-carpet-bombing media coverage of last year's Summer Games caused me to reflect on how much – and how quickly – the world has changed since my now-distant youth. Thirty-six years ago as a 4th grader, I watched, captivated, as American decathlete Bruce Jenner won a gold medal in the Montreal Olympics, earning him the title of "World's Greatest Athlete," and 7 years of face-time on Wheaties cereal boxes. Now he's a punch line on a flaky TV show. What happened to the allure of the decathlete? And how did it happen so fast?

**Don't Turn That English Channel**

**What's transpired since Montreal** is nothing short of a seismic historic tipping point, with mankind experiencing the greatest proliferation of individuals and information our planet has ever seen. Since 1976, civilization has spawned an unprecedented growth in humans and hardware, with our population surging from 4 billion to over 7 billion, while the amount of data and knowledge created and captured has grown exponentially beyond even that. By eliminating most of the debilitating viruses hampering both computers and communities, the collective, unbridled force of the human intellect has finally been realized on a global scale. That's the GOOD news. The BAD news is that now, in order to truly stand out and succeed as an athlete, employee, company, or country, we have no choice but to specialize and focus on showcasing the individual strengths that make us unique, for the simple mathematical reason that we are now competing with a staggering number of competitively-priced alternatives available within the worldwide marketplace, and the sheer breadth and depth of mankind's surging knowledgebase can no longer be mastered by a single person.

In June 2012, the Harvard Business Review website published a guest blog by Dr. Vikram Mansharamani entitled "All Hail the Generalist," celebrating and championing the superior value of generalists in today's world. I know he has a doctorate, with degrees from Yale and MIT, but in this case – he's wrong. In our flat-earth ecosystem of increasing specialization and connectivity, where tens of thousands of people are considered "one in a million," neither the sports world nor the business world will accommodate those decathletes or generalists that don't fit neatly inside their depth charts or org charts (a condition which is now bubbling up and impacting the brand of America as a nation). What follows is a rebuttal of Vikram's premise, featuring a robust substantiation of our new era defined by specialization, and finishing with a challenge to, in fact, "Double Down" on our nationwide commitment to championing the power and impact of a laser-like focus on specialized core competencies within our citizenry.

**Do You Believe in Magic?**

**In Game 6 of the 1980 NBA finals,** Magic Johnson famously played all five positions for the LA Lakers, netting 42 points, 15 boards, 7 assists, and 3 steals in a winning cause against the 76'ers. Nobody has come close to this accomplishment since then. Why? Specialization. At 6'9" and 255, Magic was able to compete with anyone on the floor back then, and his numbers back it up. Not anymore. In an era when LeBron James at 6'8" 255 is considered a "Small Forward," and where athletic centers over 7' are common, it's clear that the versatility required to match up with the unique requirements to play every position on the floor is no longer possible, and the athletes that attempt this are destined for disappointment.

A classic example of this phenomenon is evidenced by the fleeting and frustrating career of Pittsburgh Steelers quarterback Kordell Stewart. Nicknamed "Slash," Kordell came into the league as the prototype for the "Quarterback of the Future," combining the best of a traditional pocket passer with the quick-feet option of a running back, should the play break down. On paper, Slash's value proposition was to give teams a "2 for 1" benefit – traditional downfield passing integrated with elusiveness and the ability to scramble, salvage plays, and make something out of nothing. A brief review of his career reveals a sad commentary and an unfortunate outcome. In spite of being ranked 6th on the list of the 10 most versatile players in NFL history (and ranking second only to Steve Young's 43 rushing TD's), Slash played every season "on the bubble," knowing he was always one game away from being benched in favor of a more traditional quarterback, who fit better into a linear, predictable and established offensive system. Whereas Slash saw his skills as "the best of both worlds," coaches saw ambiguity and risk, as he was never as good as the best PURE drop-back passers, and never as good as the best PURE running backs.

A decade after Slash was unceremoniously cut from his last team, a new generation of hybrid players like Tim Tebow – who dare to challenge the historical mold of the quarterback position – continue to be faced with pushback and resistance from coaches who can't get their heads around how to use his many talents. In spite of his demonstrated leadership, clutch performance, and nerves of steel required to WIN

GAMES throughout his entire career, it seems all team owners want to talk about are his unorthodox mechanics, slow release, or other reasons to relegate him to obscure 3rd down options, or the occasional "Wildcat" formation to keep defenses honest. Rather than try to design an offense to capitalize on his unique breadth of talent, they continue to try and force-fit him into their predictable preconceived notions of a quarterback playing "inside the box."

The lessons from Slash and Tebow are clear. In an era where athletes are groomed exclusively for short yardage situations, killing power plays, or throwing 9 pitches to close out the 9th inning, you'd better decide who you want to be – and specialize – or you're going to be out of work and/or permanently "on the bubble," and vulnerable to the "less risky" alternative of other athletes who have committed to branding themselves with an exclusive and specialized skill set.

## From Peking Man to Vitruvian Man to Pac-Man

**Since the dawn of time,** humans have specialized in discrete trades, becoming blacksmiths, cobblers, and farmers, and have passed these skills down through the generations in order to survive (I've heard even sorcerers had apprentices). However, for the past 500 years, there has been a cultural counter-movement suggesting that it was possible, and in fact desirable, to be a generalist. In 1487, Leonardo da Vinci created a pen and ink drawing of "Vitruvian Man," exemplifying the perfect blend of art and science, and demonstrating his belief and commitment to proportion in all things. Just as Michelangelo's David was considered the ideal human specimen in terms of physical prowess, de Vinci's Vitruvian construct quickly became the archetype for the intellectual ideal, and it was this integrated image that went on to champion the Renaissance narrative celebrating the pursuit and mastery of a broad knowledgebase spanning music, science, art, languages, and even athletics.

500 years later – and shortly after Pac-Man was introduced – the explosion in both our worlds' total population and technological productivity forever thwarted the ability of a single person to acquire the breadth of knowledge necessary to master mankind's amassed intellectual genius, and the mega-trend of reverting BACK to specialization began its rapid acceleration.

## Liberal Arts: Great for the Renaissance – Lousy for the Recession

**A few years ago,** *Parade* magazine featured an exchange asking, "Why are the arts considered liberal, as in liberal arts?" The piece went on to describe that "liberal" in this context has nothing to do with politics, but rather harkens back centuries, originating from the root word "liberty," and used to describe work or studies that one undertook freely, in contrast to activity necessary to earn a living or train for a technical job or profession.

Do you see the problem? Thousands of colleges and universities are stuck in a Renaissance-era time-warp, featuring liberal arts curricula and degrees, and graduating millions of massively indebted generalists who are studying topics that, frankly, should only have been pursued if their families were independently wealthy, and this educational pursuit was simply a way to expand their intellectual horizons during their hours of leisure.

The resulting human tragedy is as sad as it is predictable; a depressing, slow-motion, years-long, unfolding realization by students (and their parents) of the pronounced disconnect between the degree they've invested in, and what the market now requires to get a meaningful job. But by then it's too late. In hindsight, it turns out that instead of waxing poetic about "studying the classics" and parroting back the Kool-Aid induced "benefits of a broad-based education" pedagogy, they should have been refining their focus and using that time to train for a specialized profession. The simple, painful lesson a generation of graduates have learned is that the underpinning philosophy of this kind of generalized education is perfect – as long as there's no pressure or requirement to translate it into gainful employment or income.

### Admissions of an Admissions Counselor

**How many times** have you heard peppy, preppie, lapel-pin-sporting, edgy-eyeglass-wearing, lanyard-noosed college recruiters coo in cult-like unison,

"We're looking for well-rounded students." This catch-phrase is so overused, that even calling it cliché would be cliché. The fact is, colleges ARE looking for well-rounded students, but here's what they DON'T tell you – most employers AREN'T! Therefore, unless graduates have no need to translate their education into gainful employment, it is incumbent upon college students to execute a strategy for quickly transitioning from well-rounded (broad and shallow) to specialized (narrow and deep) in the course of their four years of higher education.

**Union Jack of All Trades**

**As we've already established,** there's no such thing as a "jack of all trades" anymore, because today there are just too many trades! Case in point. When I completed undergrad back in the '80's, I began a fledgling career in something called "Information Technology." Believe it or not, I.T. was actually considered a vertical back then, alongside other fields like real estate, banking, and healthcare. Three decades later, "technology" has grown so ubiquitous that it isn't so much a vertical as a "horizontal," enabling every other industry, and now considered more an invisible "hygiene factor" (supporting organizational plumbing) than as a discrete industry unto itself. Within the span of my brief career, the quality and quantity of the world's technological infrastructure and knowledge base has "Moore's Lawed" so fast, that telling people "I work in Information Technology" is now almost meaningless, as I.T. now impacts the livelihood of such a great proportion of professionals, within an increasing array of industries and specialty areas.

## Resistance is Feudal

**The era of trying to be** "all things to all people" is over, and nowhere is this more evident than in today's competitive job market. The executive career site NETSHARE featured a great article by CEO Katherine Simmons in which she writes:

"I've had many engaging, fascinating and frustrating, conversations with NETSHARE members seeking new positions. They usually have broadly eclectic resumes and diverse skill sets, which make them great conversationalists but hard to pin down when it comes to a specific next career move. When asked what, specifically, they are looking I hear things like, "a new challenge" or "I don't want to relocate" (while) the inevitable response is "I'm open to anything." When we tried to nail down specific roles, it was the same: "Oh, I have skills in that area – I can handle that."

**Wrong answers.** The age of the Renaissance man is past. This is the age of specialization, like it or not, and you need to proactively present yourself as the ideal candidate for a specific task to be considered. Too often, executive job searchers seem to have lost their way in this regard, and they see their experience as applicable in so many areas. All of them have "been there, done that," but that doesn't mean they are qualified for every job that touches their experience. It's critical to focus, to make a choice as to what role, specifically, you want. It's not enough to say, "I want a leadership role" or "P&L responsibility." You need to be prepared to define what your career goals are so recruiters and hiring managers can put you in the right context. You need to be prepared to say, "I want to be CTO of a leading software company that delivers enterprise database technology to Fortune 500 companies," or "I want to be the best sales manager selling HVAC products in the Northeast."

I couldn't have said it better myself.

### Want to Get Hired? Think Inside the Box

**Positioning yourself as a generalist** in today's work world is career suicide (e.g. Slash, Exhibit A) because it makes the fundamentally flawed assumption that employers will have the insight to interpret your breadth and versatility as a value-added benefit, bringing a fresh, valuable, and diverse perspective to their organization, instead of viewing you as a non-traditional and risk-laden compromise that fails to perfectly align with the rigid parameters of their corporate system. The fact is, firms have spent a LOT of time creating wonderfully detailed org charts, comprised of hundreds of little boxes, and each containing its own narrow, detailed, and specific list of duties. When one of these org chart boxes is added or vacated, firms then advertise the opening, and equip their HR staff with sophisticated screening tools and search engine scripts to ensure that only those candidates with the exact credentials and precise career path described are considered for these positions.

To get hired, or to even pass successfully through the screening sieve, candidates must have an increasingly deep domain skill set in the primary area of expertise outlined in the companies' job description. (Note: Don't kid yourself. All of the "soft skills" in the world won't matter if you don't have the key "hard skills" required). But here's the kicker. Whereas "Computer programmer with 5 years of I.T. experience" may have been sufficiently specific in the 80's and many candidates would have qualified, today's descriptions slice and splice an increasingly intricate litany of skills and experiences, such that job listings now resemble real estate listings.

So here's the question. Should we hate companies for their discriminating requirements? Absolutely not! Why? Because these skills are essential to perform the job AND because there are people out there with sufficiently high levels of specialization who meet these criteria. Over the past few decades, state-of-the-art technology has become so advanced, nuanced, and powerful, that mastery requires a concerted amount of effort, focus, and specialization to ensure the entirety of the feature set is explored and maximum value is extracted, and this goes not just for computers but for scores of other advanced devices in an array of industries.

## The Farmer in the Dell (Computer)

**In the July 2012 edition** of *The Atlantic*, author Chrystia Freeland proclaims, "Farming is in the midst of a startling renaissance – one that holds lessons for America's economic future," before continuing:

"The rural renaissance isn't just a curiosity: it's an important new chapter in the story of America's ability to thrive in the global economy, and in eras of disruptive technological change. As America struggles to adapt to a new wave of creative destruction that is shaking up the manufacturing and service sectors as profoundly as industrialization transformed the agrarian age, the resurgence of the family farm offers some lessons on how we might survive this wave of change. At the heart of the farm boom are the very same forces that are remaking the rest of the American economy – technological revolution and global integration…but one source of rural prosperity is the adoption of radical new technologies – and a consequent surge in productivity."

The article notes that prior to World War II, it took 100 hours of labor to produce 100 bushels of corn – but now it takes less than two – which means that Freeland's father can now farm his entire 3,200-acre homestead with the help of just two other workers, while earning revenue in excess of $2M in the process. Freeland continues, "Large-scale farmers today are sophisticated businesspeople who use GPS equipment to guide their combines, biotechnology to boost their yields, and futures contracts to hedge their risk. They are also pretty rich."

**As it turns out,** the advanced computer systems powering their gargantuan $520,000 combines, "Have been programmed with the exact parameters of the fields and are synched up with one another. That means the seed drill knows what last year's harvest was from each inch of land, thanks to data recorded by the combine, and can seed and apply fertilizer accordingly," not to mention leveraging IntelliCruise to automatically speed up or slow down depending on how heavy the crop is.

Freeland's article exploring the impact of advanced technology on farming is a perfect proxy for nearly every other industry, as it details how the integration of computers, science, and machinery have had a pronounced force multiplier effect, allowing farmers to do more with less. The positive economic upside of this bouillabaisse of innovation is achieving unprecedented levels of productivity and profit. The accompanying socio-economic downside is the surge of displaced workers, whose muscly brawn has been replaced by mechanized brains.

Freeland concludes that the only solution to this two-edged sword – which I've taken to calling the "Productivity Dividend" – is a commitment to deep, advanced, and specialized education. This knowledge set should include customized education for workers who remain on the farms – empowering them with the training and tools required to manage a high-tech

3,200-acre business (and running machinery costing more than a McMansion) – AND education in other equally specialized industries for those farm-hands no longer needed, due to the industry-wide advancements in science, technology, and productivity.

## Bend it Like Buckingham

**The quickest way** to solve our nations' current economic malaise is to focus on how to best reconcile America's Productivity Dividend. And the fastest way to fix America's Productivity Dividend is through a strategic focus on educating millions of Americans – not to be generalists – but to master specific advanced tools and technologies – a solution which will create the double benefit of increased productivity combined with decreased unemployment.

How do I know this? It's through the hard cold journalism of *USA Today*. On July 4, 2012, *USA Today* featured a column by Richard Haass and Klaus Kleinfeld in which they reported that even with high unemployment levels, over 300,000 manufacturing jobs continue to go unfilled because employers are unable to find workers, "With the advanced math, science, and technology skills that modern manufacturers need." They go on to note that, "Manufacturing employs 12 million people in jobs that provide pay and benefits well above the national average (and) account for more than 10% of the country's economy and 68% of its research and development investments." To help reconcile this disconnect, businesses like Alcoa have formed partnerships with community colleges in SC, TN, and VA, and other large firms have signed up for the "Skills for America's Future Program," a new federal initiative to foster partnerships between companies and community colleges.

While the article includes some positive suggestions like establishing common standards, creating industry-endorsed training programs giving graduates nationally-recognized and portal skills, and creating an online database linking students, community colleges, and employers, the over-arching takeaway was summed up in their resigned conclusion that, "Today's manufacturers often rely on precision machinery, computer modeling, and high-tech tooling far removed from the traditional assembly line, and too few American students are prepared for these skilled, internationally competitive jobs."

At the risk of redundancy, I might paraphrase their conclusion to read, "Too many generalists – not enough specialists," while at the same time bristling at the innuendo and disrespectful subtext contained in the fact that all of these initiatives are currently focused at the "community college" level. I find it amazing that in the midst of a generational mega-trend AWAY from generalists, that there remains a national, ongoing and fundamental misunderstanding of the widening rift between the expensive, 4-year liberal arts degrees being earned by students and where the ACTUAL market demand for the next wave of human capital resides.

## Time for Tough Love

**Let me put it** as simply as I can. For thousands of years, farmers have used primitive plows and tools, but now they use high-tech tractors and equipment to maximize productivity. Unfortunately, our current university system continues to graduate millions of students with a broad-based education featuring the farming equivalent of a fluency in pitchfork, hoe, and horsemanship, whereas employers need someone with a biotech proficiency, refined computer skills, and with a Class B license who can start driving their $520,000 combine next week…and students still can't figure out why they aren't getting hired. Employers in a variety of fields are rightfully asking (the equivalent of), "Why should I have to pay to teach you how to drive a combine and prepare you for my industry – shouldn't colleges do that? In fact, what WERE you doing for 4 years? Couldn't you take a semester to at least get certified in something? You spent $100K and still have no specific skills that can immediately add value to my firm. It's like showing up to class without doing your homework." And students are wondering, "Why didn't anyone tell me this before I got a degree in Philosophy?"

On July 10, 2012, *CNNMoney* featured an article in which the Organization for Economic Cooperation and Development (OECD) warned that the ongoing jobs crisis could permanently damage the economic prospects of the world's youngest workers, and have a "scarring effect" on their long-term career paths and future earnings prospects. According to recent statistics, last year 14.8% of U.S. workers aged 15 to 24 were neither employed, nor in school or training programs, prompting OECD to continue to "Urge employers and policymakers to create more work-study programs, including internships and other vocational training programs to address the problem." So, how do you avoid becoming a 24-year-old statistic? Start planning when you're 15!

**Polaris: A Guiding Star**

**Ask any of your astronomer friends** about Polaris, and they'll tell you that it's the brightest star in the constellation Ursa Minor, that it also responds to names such as the Pole Star, Lodestar, or North Star, and that its greatest legacy has been serving as history's Guiding Star, helping the lost chart their path to safety. Here in the Cleveland area, Polaris is also the name of a progressive career center ideally positioned to serve as the archetype for a refreshingly relevant educational model tackling head-on the challenge of educating a SPECIALIZED world-class workforce, by implementing a proactive, holistic, and integrated approach for seamlessly transitioning students "from teenager to team leader."

Polaris' entire outcomes-based ecosystem is predicated on one elegant, simple, and unapologetically pragmatic objective – to gain skills for gainful employment. By taking a strategic career approach and methodically mapping out a 3-8 year time horizon, high school juniors are able to begin specializing as young as 16, and begin taking courses in their field which earn both high school and college credits, while preparing for industry-recognized certifications, connecting with business apprenticeship and internship programs, and mingling with the exact firms seeking their exact skills. The end result is that by age 22, when others are just out of college wondering how to write their resume, get noticed, and start their career, graduates of this program could not only have a 4-year degree, but also 3-5 years of specialized, hands-on training, a network of industry contacts, and the added benefit of "immediate employability" because every step on their journey has been leading towards the same outcome – specialization – with an emphasis on mastering and leveraging high force multiplier technologies to maximize America's Productivity Dividend.

Just as Polaris is called the Guiding Star, so this focused, integrated approach enables high school students to begin mapping out a pathway for obtaining the necessary skills, certifications, degrees and instruction to guide them towards a rewarding career in a targeted niche, and featuring skillsets that employers can immediately recognize and use.

### Boston University Throws a "Special-Tea" Party

**Contrary to Dr. Mansharamani's opinion,** the tectonic shift from generalist to specialist has become so blindingly obvious that even glacier-paced, post-secondary educational establishments are beginning to break rank, as forward-thinking schools – and students – realize that the emperor has no clothes, and a general liberal arts diploma is no longer sufficient to guarantee passage to that elusive upper-middle-class lifestyle, which was once the bartered reward for the cost and commitment of a bachelors degree.

In a recent *Poets & Quants* article, journalist John Byrne describes how Boston University's new Dean Kenneth Freeman is transforming this once overlooked Boston stepchild into a progressive, cutting-edge institution by throwing out the dated, dusty, and generic "studying the classics" curriculum and instead committing to emphasizing domain expertise in discrete, specialized, and high-impact growth areas. The Freeman leadership team has determined that over the next 5, 10, and 20 years, there will be more job creation, more financial market creation, and more value creation for societies, communities, and countries in healthcare/life sciences, digital technology, and alternative energy and sustainability, so those are going to be the three primary branches of study. According to Freeman, "We're recruiting for specific disciplines but we are also doing it with a twist by focusing on specialization in digital technology, the health sector, and energy. For us to be distinguished, we have to have cutting-edge research in these fields," and so, "We are transforming our case content to reflect these sectors much more so than the traditional sectors of the past."

## Law Schools Press Charges ... Onto Students

**The deafening drumbeat** marching us from generalist to specialist is now extending all the way to those "safe" careers that had historically been insulated from the impact of economic downturns. In a June 14, 2012 interview conducted by Bloomberg Law's Lee Pacchia, University of Colorado law professor Paul Campos reveals that according to the most recent NALP statistics, only 1 in 3 law school graduates from the Class of 2011 ended up with a real legal job nine months after graduation, while the cost of law school has quadrupled over the past generation to nearly $150K (even as wages have deteriorated) – effectively making them indentured servants to the U.S. Treasury, as their debt cannot be discharged in bankruptcy. Because massive online databases now contain countless case studies, legal contracts, and "cut and paste" templates, the need for lower-level generalists commanding traditional attorney salaries is quickly drying up, with priority instead being placed on specialized lawyers who've acquired deep domain expertise in select verticals of growing demand. His conclusion is that we now require an enormous structural correction wherein society produces half the number of law school graduates at half the tuition price. He insightfully identifies this industry as simply a "canary in the coal mine" for the much larger trend permeating our broader society, warning, "We have a large class, a whole generation, of highly educated young people who have nothing they can do that really justifies either the cost or the effort that they have put into in acquiring higher education. That's a recipe for social turmoil."

The poignancy of Campos' point is consistent with the June 8, 2012 Forbes.com article "Best and Worst Master's Degrees for Jobs" by Jacquelyn Smith, quoting Payscales's lead economist Katie Bardaro, "In a technology driven world, the need for those who not only understand, but can improve upon technology is high." Bardaro continues, "As businesses of all types depend upon technology to get things done, computer science degree-holders will remain in high demand. Electrical engineering, physics and economics degrees also make the top 10, all with an average mid-career salary of more than $110,000 a year. A master's in business administration (MBA) can also earn you six figures mid-career—but because of the poor growth outlook for common jobs held by these degree-holders, it doesn't make the top 10 list."

### It's Man Versus Machine

**If lawyers and MBA's aren't safe** from the global paradigm shift from generalist to specialist – than who is? Apparently nobody. In fact, it appears that the very machines created to make life easier have turned against us. In an effort to separate fact from fiction in today's job search trenches, Wharton professor Peter Cappelli documented in his recent piece "Software Raises Bar for Hiring," the story of a Philadelphia-area HR executive who applied anonymously for a job in his own company as an experiment – and didn't even make it through the screening process. Cappelli was not surprised, noting that "It is part of a long-term trend, and the recession caused employers to be pickier, to get even more specific in the skills they think they can find outside the company and cut back on training," reinforcing again the necessity for a renewed cultural emphasis on focusing, specializing, and advanced training.

In his book "Why Good People Can't Get Jobs," he contends, "If the chief problem is one of too many workers and not enough jobs, then today's unemployment is treatable and there's a case for more fiscal and monetary policy to stimulate demand. But if the problem is chiefly a mismatch between skills employers need and those the jobless have, then more fiscal and monetary medicine won't do much good." Unfortunately, in our increasingly keyword driven, automated, and algorithmic environment, employers have little to lose by opportunistically seeking "unicorns" – those one-in-a-million candidates possessing all 30 of their specific job requirements, and yet who is – amazingly – available. Because the best defense is a good offense, the most effective way to combat this phenomenon is for job seekers to continually focus on expanding the depth (versus the breadth) of their skill set, to improve their chances of making the short list.

## Legendary Retailer Couldn't Sear Around the Corner

**If I asked you to describe** the Sears brand in 3 words, what would you say? In 1893, Richard Sears partnered with Alvah Roebuck to create Sears, Roebuck and Co., and quickly became an American success story, famous for their iconic 525-page mail order catalog featuring everything from sewing machines and sporting goods, to archery equipment and automobiles. Now, 120 years later, Sears is an American tragedy, and part of a growing list of what I call "Walk Through" stores – those retailers shoppers seek out for their empty parking lots, and then "Walk Through" on their way to more desirable and specialized stores in the mall.

## From Iconic to Ironic

**What's ironic about Sears'** "rags to riches…to rags" story is that the very novelty that, for a century, was considered a value-add – having every product imaginable under one roof – in our new era of specialization has become a corporate death sentence, and the precipitous drop in Sears' stock price from $188 in 2007 to $55 in 2012 shows just how damaging this failure to focus is to their bottom line. Amazingly, it was the very same variety and breadth of offerings that distanced Sears from their competitors that has now become the millstone drowning their fortunes. Within a single generation, their vision of a "General

Store" went from being a brand differentiator to a brand disaster, as consumers became confused, overwhelmed and ambivalent towards a merchandizer that sold everything from lawn mowers to lingerie. Their sudden desperate merger with Kmart in 2008 was merely an admission of failure, as these two generational generalists lunged at each other with all the synergy and grace of a drunken bar fly and a grizzled bartender realizing they're the only ones left in the tavern at 2am.

Like Sears, retail peer J.C.Penny is coming to the realization that in our worldwide pendulum swing toward specialization, a failure to focus is a failure to succeed, and even draconian measures to reimagine, rebrand, and repackage "general offerings" to the general public are met with yawns – and a stock price plummet from $43 to $19 in the past 6 months. But it's even worse than that. From 2007 – 2012, General Electric's stock price dropped from $42 to $20, General Dynamics dropped from $94 to $64, and General Motors dropped from $39 to $19 (in the past 18 months). Do you see the pattern? The global specialization trend has become so pronounced, that simply having the word "General" in your company name is enough to decimate the market value of your company. In fact, even industry powerhouse Best Buy (which has watched its stock drop from $48 to $19 in the past two years) is realizing that their product mix selling servers and stoves, vacuums and video games, and dryers and DVDs – even though they're all "electronic" – is still not sufficiently focused and specialized to ensure a sustainable competitive advantage in the marketplace.

## IBM: An American Case Study

**In his book,** "The Measure of a Nation: How to Regain America's Competitive Edge," author Howard Friedman argues that if America today were a corporation, it would be the equivalent of IBM in the early 1990's. He writes, "IBM had dominated the technology space for decades but it lost its lead in the 1980s as it outsourced key elements to competitors. Those competitors soon became mega-companies, while IBM slipped. By the end of the decade, IBM was overstaffed and overinvested in low-margin business; revenue had peaked in 1990 and was declining rapidly while its profit margins and stock price plummeted."

What IBM did next shocked the world. They took an objective and critical look at their company compared to the rapidly changing technology industry and asked, "What is our core competency, what do we do better than anyone else, and how can we leverage these strengths to maintain a profitable business and sustain our competitive advantage in an increasingly global marketplace?" Once this question was honestly asked and honestly answered, the solution was obvious – specialize!

Rather than continue to feature a broad base of business and technology offerings, IBM chose to sell their legacy PC business to Lenovo in 2005 (thereby ending their exhausting, resource-intensive, and ultimately losing battle for razor-thin hardware margins in a race to the bottom), and instead focused on developing and growing their high-value, high-margin, and high-profile business software and consulting services. By strategically choosing to become more specialized and occupy a narrower but deeper market niche, IBM has not only succeeded in becoming more dominant in terms of intellectual property (holding more patents than any other U.S.-based technology company), but also stronger financially, featuring increasing margins, significant free cash flow, and nearly 50% in recurring revenue–exceeding even Apple in Earnings Per Share (EPS) growth on a multiple basis.

### Apple: An American Success Story

**Learning from IBM's successful strategy** of jettisoning their low margin efforts and instead focusing on their highly profitable, highly cerebral, consulting and software solutions, Apple Inc. has effectively replicated this model with the launch of their ground-breaking iPhone and iPad, and watched their stock skyrocket from $350 to $600 over the past 12 months. A cursory look on the back of these devices reveals a simple embossed message, "Designed by Apple in California. Assembled in China," and yet within these words are contained both an elegantly straightforward synopsis of their strategy AND a blueprint for global businesses going forward.

Apple as a company has chosen to define its brand as synonymous with providing superior user experiences by introducing high-design, high-style, and high-functioning technology devices – tools which are comprised of creativity and componentry. By compartmentalizing the discrete tasks of design and assembly, Apple has chosen to specialize, defining its business and core competencies on ITS terms, and enabling them to enjoy the best of both worlds – a high-end, high-margin, high-value-add, highly confidential, highly talented design/creative/leadership workforce in the U.S., AND low-cost, mass-produced, low-value-add, low-vulnerability assembly in China.

## Of Business and Barbells

**Both Apple and IBM** have demonstrated the financial benefits of prioritizing high-value-add strategies, and proven that change is possible. However, their experiences clearly demonstrate it won't "just happen" automatically, as the inertia of legacy policies and positioning will always require a concerted effort to redirect.

A recent article by Dan Zehr entitled, "Midlevel Jobs Vanishing From Marketplace" affirms the "Apple Trend" described above, noting the increasing hollowing out of the middle tier of the job market over the past three decades. Zehr writes that, "The real bulk of the job growth is bubbling up at the ends of the spectrum – in low-pay, low-skill jobs and in higher-wage, highly skilled occupations that more and more often require at least a four-year college degree." The article attributes this barbell effect to the replacement of clerical tasks by information technology, and the replacement of manufacturing tasks by robotic technology. His conclusion (are you ready?) is that the job force must obtain increasingly specialized skills in order to operate the technologies that are powering these productivity gains – or get permanently left behind in low-skilled, low-paying positions.

## What Apple Can Teach America About Core Competency

**When Americans see** "Designed by Apple in California, Assembled in China" on their iPod, or hear about Ralph Lauren designing our Olympians' uniforms in the U.S. (but having them sewn in China), we can either scream until we're red, white, and blue in the face, OR we can channel that passion towards figuring out a strategy for not only surviving but thriving in our evolving global economy. America as a nation no longer has the luxury of resting on its laurels or continuing business as usual, and it's clear our economy is not going to be saved by Europe (6 nations falling into recession), China (GDP at a 3 year low), Washington, or Wall Street (fiscal cliff, debt ceiling, Operation Twist, QE Useless). This time, it's up to us. With the fate of our nation in the balance, the hour has come for someone to step up and take a big-tent approach towards positioning the brand of America for the next 100 years, and since nobody else has stepped forward, I've decided to take on the challenge myself.

### The Power of Pruning: Less is More

**As a cultural anthropologist** and industry provocateur, I've learned that a brand isn't something you create, it's something you uncover. But how do you brand a nation of 330 million people? The same way IBM did with their 430,000 employees. Or, if you prefer, we could simply apply the same time-honored strategy we were taught in Driver's Ed – The IPDE Process – Identify, Predict, Decide, and Execute (Identify core competencies, Predict the future competitive landscape, Decide the best positioning, and Execute).

Believe it or not, the first step in this process – Identify core competencies – is actually the hardest, simply because in order for the BEST brand story to win, lesser brand stories have to lose. Over the years, I've had the opportunity to write and implement eight business plans, and have found that the process of deciding and declaring what you DO as a company comes with the added benefit of also determining what you DON'T do. As we've already discussed, "America the General" is no longer an option, and so – just like IBM 20 years ago – we need to focus, and honestly ask ourselves, "What is our core competency, what do we do better than anyone else, and how can we leverage these strengths to maintain a profitable economy and sustain our competitive advantage in an increasingly global marketplace?

## The United Brand of America

**The brand of America,** the soul of our nation, the DNA of the USA, is our unparalleled combination of break-through innovation AND our break-out entrepreneurs. Our patent-makers and risk-takers. The secret sauce for expanding American exceptionalism is a national commitment to architect an integrated ecosystem which supports and rewards our capitalistic call to greatness, and provides the tools, talent, technology, and terms for directly investing in this vision of our future.

## Creating Jobs Like Jobs

**Jim Clifton,** the CEO of Gallup and author of "The Coming Jobs War" offers a referendum on this vision, arguing that it's up to entrepreneurs to save America, and exhorting, "The U.S. has to keep creating, as it has in the past, the next big things and selling them. Everybody's been talking about the late Steve Jobs. You see, Steve Jobs wasn't meeting needs; his company never met a need. Steve Jobs and his company created a need. I wish all of America could get an A on this pop quiz because it's so important: China fills needs; Steve Jobs created needs. Nobody knew they needed an iPhone. The same thing was true with the transistor and flight and Henry Ford's mass production of cars. The country that invents the future wins the jobs war, and inventing the future is what great entrepreneurs do. But China's just meeting already-existing needs. They're filling orders. They don't create the future."

Every industry – from cars to clothes to computers – has entry-level, mid-tier, and high-end premium offerings. Why not decide as a nation to double down on our commitment to thought leadership and world class innovation, emphasize the exclusivity of our national brand, target the worlds' wealthiest and most discriminating buyers, and make "Made in America" recognized universally as synonymous with the best quality on the planet? We know it's going to be a barbell global economy anyway, so why not "Do like Apple" and focus on building a high-end, high-quality, high-margin, high-value-add, highly confidential, highly talented design/creative/leadership workforce in the U.S., and leave the low-cost, low-margin, low-value-add commodities for the rest of the world to fight over?

**MSN Money recently published** an article entitled, "The 10 Products America Makes Best" and highlighting the list were world-class products and iconic brands that make me proud to be an American, including Harley Davidson motorcycles, Viking/Wolf/Sub-Zero luxury kitchen appliances, Zippo brand lighters, the world's best weapons systems and defense industry, software by Apple,

Microsoft, Oracle, Symantec, Adobe, Gibson guitars, Steinway pianos, blockbuster Hollywood movies (including 87 of the 100 highest grossing movies of all time), and finally (are you sitting down?) Herman Miller chairs.

The 100-year question is, "How can we create more American success stories like these, and grow this list from 10 to 10,000?" The answer is – guys like Doug Tatum.

**A Capital Idea**

**Doug Tatum** is to the small private equity industry what Harriet Tubman was to the Underground Railroad. He lives it, he loves it, and he passionately crusades to help as many firms as possible successfully navigate the inevitable wilderness phase that every growing firm must endure if they are to achieve the size and scale necessary to realize long-term growth and profitability.

Of the roughly 1 million new U.S. small businesses started each year, 80% fail within five years, and 96% fail within ten. Because the innovators and entrepreneurs that drive small business have always been the heart, soul, and strength of our nation, the best way for securing America's future is to ensure that more of these SMALL businesses survive and grow into BIG businesses – and Doug Tatum has figured out how.

In his industry bestseller, *No Man's Land*, Tatum provides a roadmap for getting organizations successfully through corporate adolescence – that phase when firms are "Too big to be small, and too small to be big" – detailing exactly how to accelerate 20 – 40 person firms through the growth curve to the personal and professional rewards on the other side. But then he takes it a step further. As Chairman of three symbiotic companies, Tatum has established a Business Concierge service whereby small businesses are walked through a "Continuum of Capital" – from Market to Management to Model to Money – thereby maximizing their chances of success. His Inc. Navigator firm (aligned with Inc. Magazine), provides an industry-specific diagnostic tool for corporate planning, along with a strategy scorecard for charting progress along the way. His Newport Board Group firm provides senior level expertise via a nationwide team of executives and domain experts, and features its Inc. Compass tool for tracking direction and milestones. And Evolution Capital Partners, "Invests exclusively in U.S.-based companies of 20 – 40 employees, led by passionate entrepreneurs generating between $500K – $2M in annual free cash flow, who are committed to transforming and growing their firms, and with the goal of reaching $5 million in free cash flow within 3-7 years."

## Continuum of Capital

**While I've never met** or spoken to him, I've chosen to feature Tatum and his model here for a variety of reasons. First, because he's clearly passionate about America, and doing what he can to improve our economic future. Second, in a world of sexy international hedge funds and elite billion-dollar private equity clubs, he's made a commitment to specialize and focus exclusively on helping those entrepreneurs overlooked by banks and brokers, who are struggling to make it in the trenches of small business. Third, because it appears he's the first person to actually connect the dots and codify a repeatable formula for helping good companies become great. His precision model has consistently proven that small, targeted, $3-$5M investments in the right firms, at the right time in their life-cycles, and with the right guidance, can quickly transform them into high-growth juggernauts, increasing jobs, margins, and revenue. And finally, because he understands the true meaning of CAPITAL, as evidenced by this excerpt from Evolution Capital Partners' website:

"Sure you need additional capital to grow your company, but thinking of capital as simply dollars is not enough. You need intellectual capital, emotional capital, relationship capital, been-there-done-that capital, best practices capital, and strategic capital. You need advice on how to best scale your company, from key hires to enterprise technology solutions, and from HR policies to insurance policies. You need high-level introductions to key clients that could take your business to the next level, expertise in selecting the right software, hardware, and infrastructure combinations, and the branding and marketing strategy required to leverage all of the emerging social media platforms available to spread your message to new audiences. In short, you need a partner who can amplify your upside growth while minimizing your downside risk, by applying proven scalable strategies to ensure you get it right the first time."

In a recent interview for "Economy Heroes," Tatum asserts, "America's unique competitive advantage is the innovation driven by its entrepreneurs, and the capital markets which support these entrepreneurs." I couldn't agree more. If the past four years have taught us anything, it's that the cyclical strategy of "throwing money at the problem" and hoping it trickles down to create new jobs won't solve the problem of our underlying structural misalignment. The solution for getting America back on track is precision investment, combined with professional insight, in targeted firms and industries, and integrated with the focused education of an increasingly specialized workforce optimized to drive the engines of innovation, parlaying our Productivity Dividend back into reinforcing our premium national brand.

## Lagflation Nation

**In the Spring of 2008,** I authored a multi-media economics eBook published online entitled, "Banks, Tanks & Angst: How Long Will America Idle?" in which I warned readers of the coming economic collapse, and included over 15 specific predictions which (unfortunately) have since come true. The central point of the book was to financially prepare people for a protracted, nationwide, economic paralysis – a condition I described as LAGFLATION – occurring when the average American income LAGS the cost of the average American lifestyle, and summed up in this closing paragraph:

"The American Economy during this period of LAGFLATION will be like 4 cars that arrive at a 4-way Stop Sign intersection at exactly the same time. Everyone is waiting for everyone else to go. People don't spend, so retailers lay off, so firms don't hire, so people go out less, so food prices go up even more, so restaurants close, so firms lay off even more, and laid off people don't spend, so they don't buy houses, so the prices of homes continue to fall, so they don't fly on airlines, so airlines go bankrupt, and on and on it goes. For the next 3-5 years, the entire nation will collectively stand around with their hands on their hips waiting for someone else to "Go first." The end result of LAGFLATION is that our country will increasingly be divided into a nation of Haves and Have-Nots. A nation of wealthy multinational financiers on Easy Street and multigenerational families living on Main Street. In the end, our nation will ultimately be defined by Wall Street and K-mart. Put them together and what do you have? Wal-Mart."

Three years before the "Occupy" movement began, it was clear that the financial pieces were already in place, and the economic trends in motion, that would ultimately bring the country to a crescendo of frustration, and to the brink of class warfare. Since this eBook was published, America has experienced an unemployment rate over 8% for 41 straight months (a rate and duration not seen since the Great Depression), the number of unemployed workers has risen to 14 million (with millions more underemployed), and we now have more Americans on food stamps (46 million) than at any point in our history. It's time to take a stand.

### "America the General" or "America the Boutique"

**With our global economy** continuing to accelerate towards an increasingly bifurcated caste system – characterized by the Haves and the Have-Nots – America and Americans now have to make a choice within this hollowed-out "barbell" construct and decide whether to focus on becoming low-cost generalists or high-end specialists. The Walmart brand represents all that the global "General Store" has to offer – cheap products, targeting cheap customers, earning cheap margins, and with a one-dimensional strategy of massive volume (and, of course, the hope that more and more people will earn less and less, and thereby become customers). Walmart is not a bad company. I shop at Walmart. But it's not the business model I wish for America or Americans.

While Walmart has its place, my desire is to see America spawn thousands of firms like 3-D printing company ExOne, which USA Today described in its July 11, 2012 edition as perfecting the process of, "Meticulously spreading hundreds or thousands of layers of powdered metal onto canvas until they form three-dimensional shapes," with multiple machines run by a single operator, and which, "Exemplifies the latest chapter of the industrial revolution, one that could make U.S. manufacturing more competitive globally and could bring more jobs back to the United States."

**The article continues,** "Since just a few employees run dozens of printers – vs. several hundred or thousands of workers in traditional factories – some experts say the technology can neutralize the low-cost labor advantage the countries such as China and India enjoy over the U.S. That, along with 3-D printing's ability to accommodate quick product launches, is expected to accelerate a nascent "reshoring" trend that has seen a growing number of manufactures bring some production back to the U.S, and it becomes very competitive with anything you can get from China," says Scott Paul, executive director of the Alliance for American Manufacturing. While 3-D printing may well mean fewer U.S. manufacturing jobs in the near term, the growing number of factories that likely will relocate to the U.S. should yield a net increase in employment. With that goal in mind, the federal government is spending $45 million to help fund a planned additive manufacturing institute that will develop innovations for the burgeoning industry and help bring it into the mainstream."

Each year, this high tech industry breaks new ground in driving down inefficiency while increasing productivity, reducing the costs and delays associated with complex or customized parts made in limited quantities (and adding no expense for multiple design changes), thereby making it ideal for surgical tools, medical implants, and things like orthodontic braces that are tailored to a patients' unique tooth structure.

**Brain Beats Brawn**

**The historic battle** of brains versus brawn has been fought – and brains have won. Computers, technology, and the advanced devices they now power enable workers to harness this "mechanical advantage," leveraging what I call a "workforce multiplier effect," and accomplishing more with less human involvement. Because of this, it is incumbent upon the workforce of the future to prioritize large-scale mastery of these cutting-edge platforms, as this represents America's best option for creating that elusive Win-Win (maximum productivity AND maximum employment) while obtaining the best reinvestment returns on our nations' Productivity Dividend.

Both IBM and Apple are clarion examples of global firms who have taken the necessary steps to successfully pivot and compete on a global stage – not by trying to be all things to all people – but by drawing a line in the sand and committing to focus on the high-margin, high-value-add, highly cerebral end of the business spectrum, and leaving the less profitable components for other countries to fight over.

The message to our nation is just as simple, and just as powerful. America's global brand, competitive differentiator, and central core competency is our world-beating innovation and entrepreneurs, working in concert with our business ecosystem that fosters creativity and ambition, and a culture which nurtures, celebrates, and enables great ideas and ingenuity to flourish.

**The message to American workers,** politicians, colleges, and companies from coast to coast is just as clear. In order to expand upon our "Made in America" global brand of excellence, we need to differentiate and specialize in those sectors and industries that are the most advanced and the most profitable. Over the next 100 years, world dominance will go to the smartest. It's Revenge of the Nerds on a global scale. Our pure labor costs seldom enable America to compete on price – so don't! Does Apple compete on price? No. Harley Davidson? No. America needs to understand that her underlying and sustaining source of brand and global competitiveness is her high-end quality and innovation, supported by ambitious entrepreneurs. Innovation and commoditization are at opposing ends of the profit spectrum. Instead of fighting with the rest of the world for undesirable scraps of business in a race to the bottom, we should follow the Apple model and perform the high-margin, innovative work here, while sourcing the mass-production where the cost equation is most advantageous (which could once again be in America, if industries like 3-D printing continue to flourish and drive down cost while driving up productivity).

The bottom line is this. If we organize around this vision, and commit to executing on this strategy by focusing our educational model AWAY from graduating generalists and TOWARDS creating generations of specialists, we push our manufacturing base, textile base, legal base, and every other base further UPSTREAM into more cerebral, intensive, and better paying jobs. In doing so on an integrated, coordinated, and national basis, our country can finally make strides towards reconciling the disconnect between educational curricula, workforce skills, and employer needs, while investing America's Productivity Dividend where it can do the most good for the greatest number of people.


### All Hail the Generalist? Hail No!

**In the last paragraph** of his piece, Dr. Mansharamani concludes, "The time has come to acknowledge expertise as overvalued." I'm sorry, but 300,000 currently unfilled manufacturing jobs say you're dead wrong. While I'm sure Dr. Mansharamani is a nice guy, and I'd probably enjoy sharing a lunch with him sometime, he simply missed the mark on this one.

(Then again, this is a man whose latest book, "Boombustology: Spotting Financial Bubbles Before They Burst," was published in 2011, three years AFTER the market crashed). In this book, he correctly observes, "We need a framework for connecting the dots in a manner that helps extract insight from the tremendous amounts of information and data that are already available," an astute observation, making it that much more ironic that in evaluating the tremendous amount of data about the state of our workforce, he came to his curious conclusion that the world needs more generalists – not less.


**Of Caveats and Caviar**

**While I wholeheartedly disagree** with Dr. Mansharamani's assessment, I'm not prepared to declare carte blanche "All FAIL the Generalist." America will always need strong leaders and generalists, those 50,000-foot thinkers who can divine the "big picture," capture data points, arrange them into patterns, extrapolate trends, and then translate, interpret, and distill these findings into actionable plans (in fact, that's what THIS document is). But remember, when America decided to take out Osama bin Laden, we didn't send in General Forces, we sent in Special Forces, deploying a Special Ops Seal Team comprised of soldiers who had invested years learning complex tactics and undergoing specialized training, precisely designed to successfully execute a challenging mission like this. In order to truly be the best of the best, you have to specialize.

Are generalists important – absolutely! In fact, I'm a generalist myself. But saying America needs to produce more generalists, is like saying the Army needs more Generals. There are currently almost 3,000,000 people serving in the U.S. Armed Forces, of which roughly 300 have reached the rank of General in the Army, and roughly 10 of those have achieved the 4-star ranking. In our Armed Forces, individuals have significantly less than a 1% chance of achieving the rank of General, and corporate American has a similar pyramid structure and leadership hierarchy. Therefore, unless you are the < 1% with the Ivy League credentials and business connections to be recruited directly from university to executive fast-track to the top tier of the pyramid, your best strategy – statistically – is to focus on developing a specific domain expertise which employers can immediately use.

## Be a Star

**On June 3, 1992,** the day after he secured the Democratic nomination, then-presidential candidate Bill Clinton appeared on the Arsenio Hall Show, donned a pair of *Risky Business* sunglasses, picked up a saxophone, and started playing "Heartbreak Hotel" with the band. At that point, you were probably thinking, "Wow, here's a guy running for President, but who also knows how to have fun, and can relate to the common man." As it turns out, this appearance was a critical moment in Clinton's political career, helping to build his popularity with minority and young voters, and leveraging the media coverage from this show to catapult him ahead of Bush in the polls, and into the White House.

With a flair for both blues and bureaucracy, one might say Bill Clinton was a broad-based generalist, a modern day Renaissance Man, BUT, I can guarantee that his LinkedIn profile back then would NOT have read, "William J. Clinton, Saxophonist & Statesman: "I put the "riffs" in "tariffs." Instead, Clinton wisely chose to specialize and focus, defining and distinguishing himself first as an attorney, and then Governor, before moving on to the Presidency. Only AFTER he had achieved a high level of success and visibility in his specialized domain did he begin to branch out and reveal some of the breadth and variety of his other skills.

A convenient metaphor for this orientation is our old friend Polaris, which, as it turns out, is a multiple star, consisting of a main star, two smaller companions, and two distant components. In today's hyper-competitive marketplace, the best strategy for effectively positioning and branding a candidate, career, company, or country is to follow the same format. Focus on a discrete, specialized, main theme, and then slowly introduce additional capabilities when appropriate, being careful not the cloud the primary core competency. For example, do you recall the moment when you discovered that Bruce Willis could sing, or that Harry Connick, Jr. could act? Once they had successfully achieved recognition in their specialized field of endeavor, this added dimension was truly a value add – a wonderful bonus surprise – which only served to make them that much more popular and endearing. The lesson here is that it's the TIMING of your branding and presentation that makes all the difference. Most everyone has a diverse set of skills, but it's best to keep your "Renaissance Man" in the closet of the "Dark Ages" until it's time to "Enlighten" the world with your many diverse gifts – at which point you are praised for your "versatility" – rather than punished for your "lack of focus." Same skills, dramatically different outcomes.

## It Takes An Olympic Village

**In conclusion,** my hope in organizing these thoughts and capturing them on paper is to give voice to this subtle but significant narrative defining our age, and, like the worldwide relay of 8,000 runners who collaborated to kick of London's Opening Ceremonies, serve as a torchbearer to spark and advance this vision, with the hope that others will consider it, internalize it, embrace it, and share it.

In the interest of levity, and in light of our current worldwide economic malaise, part of me wishes Great Britain had put a little English on the traditional Olympic decathlon events for a fort night in 2012, and replaced them with fitting challenges reflective of our contemporary financial struggle including: scaling the wall of worry, vaulting the debt ceiling, fiscal cliff diving, catching a falling knife, hurtling a value trap, swimming through a dark pool, finessing a dead cat bounce, pairs trading, support and resistance, pump and dump, JP Morgan's new whale watching event, executing a perfect operation twist (with a soft landing), and observing the storied London Bridge loans falling down. But I digress.

The message for athletes, academics, companies and countries is clear. The world no longer prefers a Swiss Army Knife – they want a drawer full of knives, each uniquely designed for a specific task.

**Your mother was right.** You ARE special. Now act like it.

## About Briarcliff Capital, LLC

Briarcliff Capital, LLC manufactures the ideas that change individuals, institutions, and industries. We're not flashy, don't follow the crowd, don't compromise the confidence of our clients, and prefer to stay under the radar. At our core, we're mavericks, and prefer to work directly with senior executives who aren't afraid to take some risk and ruffle some feathers to get results.

Briarcliff Capital is a boutique consulting company "*Integrating Principal, Principals, and Principles.*™" Our strategic forecasts and brand insights speak directly to the C-suite, with our original thought leadership content offering a refreshingly irreverent take on Wall Street, banking, economics, technology, risk, capital markets, leadership, and this nasty thing called social media. Our genre-bending style combines pithy and pragmatic, with a rapier focus on identifying not only the problem and the cause of the problem, but also the solution. Our core competency is serving as a human portal for researching, capturing, and interpreting disparate data points – whether in our economy or in a corporate environment – establishing a pattern, and then translating this pattern into actionable strategy.

Douglas O'Bryon, CEO

Briarcliff Capital, LLC
443-421-0167
dougobryon@juno.com
www.dougobryon.com

www.ingramcontent.com/pod-product-compliance
Lightning Source LLC
Chambersburg PA
CBHW071641170526
45166CB00003B/1386